WHAT IS LOVE

C.Wynanda

WHAT IS LOVE

First printing 1983

Library of Congress Catalog Card Number: 83-60672
ISBN Number: 0-912179-00-7

The photographs are for illustrative purposes
only; they do not represent the persons described
in the text.

Sonrise
Publications
4826 East Paris, S.E.
Grand Rapids, Michigan 49508

Contents

Preface

This book is the result of a lot of discussions with people in their teens and twenties on the topic of love.

Love seems to be at the center of most of our lives, especially while we're young – we talk about it, sing about it, think about it all the time, even try to plan our lives around it. But what is love exactly?

When you ask people what they think love is, the answer most of them give is that, "Well, two people just...I don't know...love each other." Whatever love is, it seems to come naturally and it seems to be important, but most people don't have a very good handle on what it really is.

There is unanimous agreement about one thing, though: none of them associates love with anything bad. Love, they all say, is a beautiful thing. Until we get around to the idea of self-love, that is. Nobody seems to have a very high opinion of that.

The trouble with defining the word *love* is that it's such a complicated idea. Our language seems to let us down here. It only gives us one word to describe both self-love and love for others. Things would be simpler if there were at least two words for these different kinds of love – but even then there would be problems. Most people find it pretty hard to draw a clear line between the different kinds of love. Maybe nobody can do it.

And that is scary. Again and again in discussions with people, the best descriptions of love always end up sounding more like self-love than anything else. That always shocks people. One girl stated she wouldn't ever be able to use the word *love* again.

Well, we can't just turn our backs on love – it's far too important a part of each of our lives. Everything we do – and everything we choose not to do – is related to motivations of one kind of love or another. We owe it to ourselves and to all the people whose lives we touch to do some serious thinking about love.

In the pages that follow, we'll be talking about some of the things that have come up in the discussions about love. It is impossible to hit on every aspect of love, of course – no one book could hope to do that – but we will try to get into areas that most people think are the most important to them as they enter the adult world.

No one will try to tell you how to live your life – you have to make your own decisions about that. But this book may help you get started thinking about love and the role you want it to play in your life. What could be more important for your future and the future of the world we'll all have to live in?

PART I
WHO HAS THE ANSWER?

Love's Definition

What Is Love?

That's a question more easily asked than answered. We've all got some gut feelings about what love is, but it's no simple matter to put it into words. Here's how one writer summed up his feelings about the subject:

*"Each to his own, and God for
   the lot—
Then everybody would get what he
   ought;
I'll make sure I get what's best,
And let God see to all the rest."*

He obviously feels that we only have two choices: we can either suffer alone or reach out and make somebody else suffer with us. There is the suggestion that the kindest thing we can do is to keep our noses out of other people's business—keep our unhappiness to ourselves.

It's easier to express your idea of love if you think it's just a losing proposition. For most of us, though, love is more complicated and valuable than that. The following teenager's definition comes closer to describing the way most of us feel about love, even if it is a little fuzzy:

"Love is a feeling that you get when you get the feeling that you've never had this feeling before."

A lot of thick books have been written about love and a lot of learned discussions have taken place that haven't gotten much closer than that to describing the nature of love. It seems as if the harder we work to nail down our thoughts about love, the farther we get from any sort of success. The most complicated explanations just end up sounding stupid.

There is one description of love that has stood the test of time, though. On one occasion its author said of himself, "What I do is not the good I want to do; no, the evil I do not want to do—this I keep on doing." The man who spoke so honestly about his own failures was Paul, a follower of Jesus Christ in the first century. He wrote with that same forthright attitude and plain language when he set out to describe his feelings about love:

"If I speak in the tongues of men and of angels, but have not love, I am only a resounding gong or a clanging cymbal. If I have the gift of prophecy and can fathom all mysteries and all knowledge, and if I have a faith that can move mountains, but have not love, I am nothing. If I give all I possess to the poor and surrender my body to the flames, but have not love, I gain nothing.

"Love is patient, love is kind. It does not envy, it does not boast, it is not proud. It is not rude, it is not self-seeking, it is not easily angered, it keeps no record of wrongs. Love does not delight in evil but rejoices with the truth. It always protects, always trusts, always hopes, always perseveres.

"Love never fails...

"And now these three remain: faith, hope and love. But the greatest of these is love." (Taken from I Corinthians 13.)

Paul has a way with words, all right. He makes love sound important – and we can agree with him on that point – but he also makes it sound next to impossible, as if it could never be a part of our ordinary lives. And yet we know that it is.

There must be another answer, but who knows what it is?

Christians claim that they know the answer. Belief in God is the answer, they say, because *God is love.*

They're really committed to that answer, too – that's why they blast the message all over the place. You hear it on the radio, and see it on T.V., and read it on billboards. Sometimes they even turn the message into a neon sign and hang it on their churches.

But is it so? Is God really love?

"No way," say a lot of people these days. "God is just a fairy tale." Superstitions like that might have been necessary in the past, when people couldn't understand the world around them any other way – and maybe there are still people around who are naive enough to need a God to make sense of the unknown – but mankind is no longer in its childhood. We've found out a few things about what makes the universe tick, and God isn't the least bit necessary."

"Besides," they go on, "even if God were real, nobody in his right mind would come to the conclusion that God is love by looking at the world. We can still smell the stench from the Nazi death camps of World War II, still feel the heat from the atomic blasts that destroyed Hiroshima and Nagasaki, still hear the cries of the slaughtered and oppressed in Vietnam, El Salvador, Afghanistan, Poland. And what about the kid we went to school with who died in a traffic accident, or the three little kids who died in the house fire reported in last night's newspaper?"

"No, if there is a God," they conclude, "it must be some kind of bad joke to say that he is love."

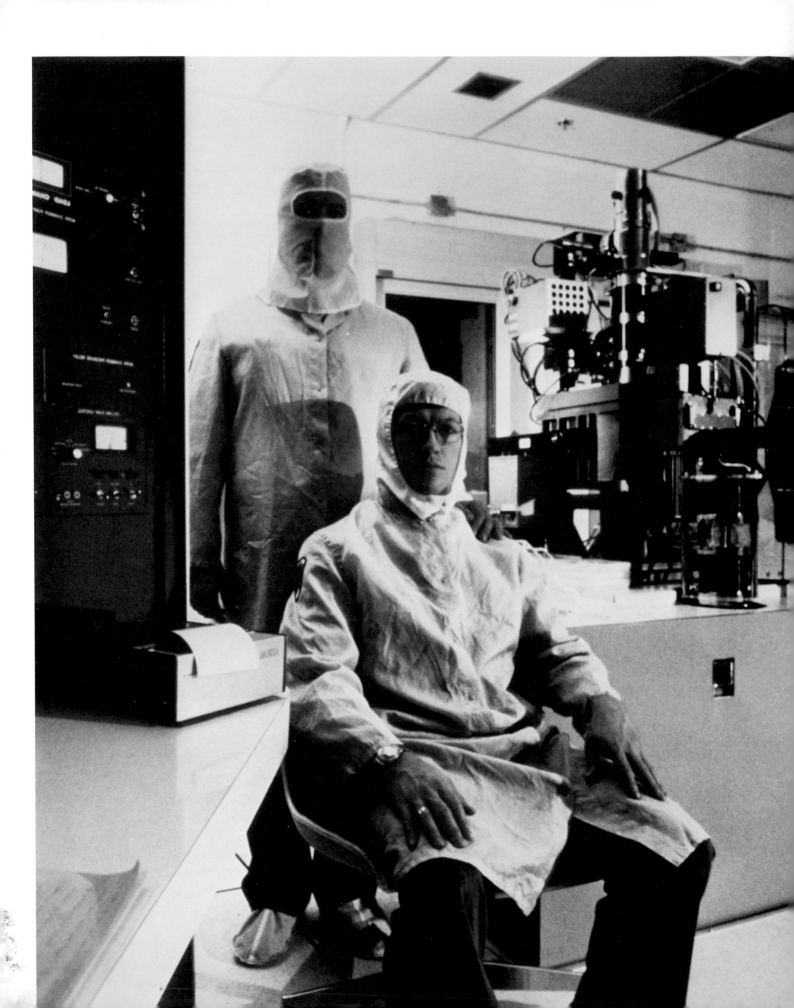

The World We Live In

It took humanity thousands of years to move from primitive nomadic cultures to the sort of complex mechanized societies that we in the Western World are used to today. The Industrial Revolution of the nineteenth century plunged our civilization into a period of furiously paced change the likes of which no previous generation had ever seen.

Scientific and technological progress have literally changed the face of the earth in addition to making it seem like a smaller place. We can now fly around the world in less time than it would have taken your grandfather to get from, say, New York City to Washington, D.C., using the fastest form of transportation that was available when he was your age.

But the question remains whether humanity's happiness has increased at the same pace with its growing technology and expanding power. We may enjoy sports cars and T.V. sets, jetliners and washing machines, air conditioners and stereo systems, but we have to remember that the same technology (and sometimes even the same companies) that made all these conveniences also produced hunter-killer satellites and rocket launchers, B-52 bombers and attack submarines, napalm and nerve gas – not to mention the ultimate weapon, the hydrogen bomb.

One of the high points of mankind's technological achievement was the moon landing in 1969. But even while the astronauts were setting foot on the lunar soil "in peace, for all mankind," the world they had left behind was embroiled in the agonies of repression and hatred and war. One world leader knelt beneath the sign of the cross while on the other side of the globe thousands of men, women, and children died horrible deaths at his command. Another world leader, speaking under the sign of the hammer and sickle, gave lip service to the rights of every individual to peace, welfare, and labor while soldiers under his command dispossessed and murdered countless thousands of his own people.

A Prayer of St. Francis of Assissi…

Lord, make me an instrument of your peace;

Where there is hatred, let me sow love;

Where there is injury, let me sow pardon;

Where there is doubt, let me sow faith;

Where there is despair, let me sow hope;

Where there is darkness, let me sow light;

Where there is sadness, let me sow joy.

O Divine Master, grant that I may not so much seek

To be consoled as to console,

To be understood as to understand,

To be loved as to love,

For it is in giving that we receive,

It is in pardoning that we are pardoned,

It is in dying that we are born to eternal life.

…And of Modern Man

O Science, make me devices to ensure my nation's peace;

Where there is hatred, give me defensive weaponry;

Where there is injury, give me anesthesia;

Where there is doubt, give me endless self-confidence;

Where there is despair, give me psychological counseling;

Where there is darkness, give me ever-brighter lights;

Where there is sadness, give me diverting entertainments.

O Technology, grant that I may find all that I seek,

That my gadgetry will always meet my needs,

That my understanding will keep pace with the latest developments,

That I might yet find love in the midst of all the machinery,

For it is in ownership that there is security,

It is in exploitation that there is progress, and

It is in dying that there will be oblivion sweeter than life.

And again we ask: *Who has the answer?*

Every step forward seems to be a step backward as well. Everything we touch seems to turn into a weapon. Progress always seems to be fatal: our technology threatens to snuff us all out, one at a time or by the millions together.

We're running out of time in which to find out what's wrong with our magnificent machines, but we have to try. We can't just throw up our arms in despair and leave the problem to somebody else. To give up the search – or even to postpone it – would be a crime.

PART II
WHERE
DO I
FIT IN?

The Search for Love in Day-to-Day Living

All You Need Is Love

Every generation searches for its own prophets, for someone to tell them the truth about the way things really stand. For a long time now, rock stars have been giving their prophetic message to a receptive audience. Rock music talks about a lot of things that are important to people. Maybe you've noticed how often the songs are about love.

The Beatles spoke to a whole generation about love, and their music is still around:

There's nothing you can do that
*   can't be done,*
Nothing you can sing that can't be
*   sung,*
Nothing you can say but you can
*   learn how to play the game –*
It's easy!
All you need is love,
All you need is love,
All you need is love, love –
Love is all you need.

A lot of years have passed since it was a hit, but the song is still around, and it still makes people smile. It's what we want to hear: "It's easy...love is all you need."

Too bad it had to end so soon. The sixties are ancient history now, the Beatles long since split up, John Lennon shot to death for no reason. Their song should have changed the world, but maybe it was *too* easy. Nobody seems to have gotten the message.

Love That Isn't Easy

The little girl pictured on the opposite page lost her arm in a tragic accident. People say she was lucky to survive, but she wonders sometimes just how lucky she really was.

Life is tough enough to face when you're healthy and whole, but a handicap like the one this girl faces can add a set of frustrations that the rest of us never begin to experience.

It's not just the problem of learning to live with an artificial arm – though of course that's no small thing in itself. The bigger problem will be learning to get along with people who feel uncomfortable about her handicap, people who show their edginess in ways that are sometimes embarrassing or rude and that are always painful.

Medical science has given her the chance to lead a normal life, but unless she also receives the concern and understanding of people around her, and musters the strength and willpower to deal with those who are less sensitive, a normal life will remain beyond her grasp.

Concern, understanding, and willpower are the essential ingredients in any loving relationship. After all, it's not likely that you'll ever really understand someone unless you're concerned enough to try. Once you do understand where the other person's coming from, though, you find it much easier to really care about him. But through it all, we're only human, and sometimes we have to rely on plain old willpower to get us through the tough situations. Love would be as weak as tissue paper if all it had was happy feelings to keep it standing: it needs the solid background of a willful determination to love the other person even when that's a difficult or unpleasant thing to do.

That kind of love isn't so easy. Some people think that it isn't possible at all. What about you? Is there anybody you'd risk anything for, anybody you'd sweat and slave to save from pain and trouble and disease? Well, there's yourself, for one.

It's a fact about human beings that we're all inclined to love ourselves to an extraordinary degree. And there's nothing really wrong with that. It even serves a practical purpose in this case, because by looking inside ourselves and exploring the depths of our love for ourselves, we can get some idea of how skimpy the love that we give to other people is by comparison.

And we can also get a feeling for the incredible task Jesus set before his followers nearly two thousand years ago when he gave the command to "Love your neighbor as yourself."

Breaking the Soil, Planting the Seed

Two different settings: on the one hand, the unbroken vista of farmland under cultivation, with bird songs and promise in the air; on the other hand, a city scene, all asphalt, concrete, and steel, packed neatly together. What's the connection?

At first glance, only contrasts are apparent. The city scene looks hard and sterile, while the open field holds the potential for life and growth in the seed that has been put into its soft, rich soil. In a few months, we might well expect, this field will be transformed into a sea of wheat or corn – or maybe weeds, if it isn't tended properly. It all depends on what's put into the soil.

The city scene contains just as much potential for life and growth as the field. Future generations are growing up behind those windows, one way or another.

What will all these new people make of the world? Who can say? Will they learn to love each other? Will they learn that they are responsible as individuals for creating peace in the world, starting with the people they meet? Will they learn to treat others with the dignity and respect they deserve? Or will they only learn to love themselves, to leave peacemaking to someone else, to respect only superior might and shrewdness?

The future of our world does not depend so much on political jousting or military strength or economic superiority. The future of the world depends on what the people behind those windows teach their children to believe.

Well, if it's true that the future
of the world depends on the things
that kids are taught to believe,
it's no wonder things are in such
a mess, right?

Most kids, especially as they
become adults, resent all the de-
mands their parents make of them.
Nobody likes being told what to do
or how to think, especially when
the values being taught are part of
a system that seems to be a failure,
judging by the wars and poverty
and exploitation it has produced.

A lot of people suspect that parents and teachers and police and
other people in authority are all in
it for the kicks – they do what they
do because they enjoy bossing
other people around. Maybe that's
true in some cases. But if you've
ever been responsible for taking
care of another person – or even
just a pet – you know that that kind
of authority isn't all fun by a
long shot.

Everybody has to pay for the
pleasures of being in authority.
Teachers have to get up in front of
classes every day and try to teach
students who often as not don't
give two hoots about what they
have to say. Police have to follow a
million rules or they'll be called on
the carpet. Parents have to sacrifice
an incredible amount of time and
money to keep their kids dressed
and fed and healthy. It's not likely
that any of them would go to that
much trouble just to be able to
boss somebody around.

People who try to blame the
lack of love in the world on problems caused by power-hungry
authority figures are looking in
the wrong place. The only way
to make sure there is more love
in the world is to add it ourselves.

Love and Fashion

In the world's celebrated fashion capitals, each season ushers in a new line of clothes. Amidst the chaos of flashbulbs and chatter, a long line of well-paid models parades the new fashions and all the important newpapers and magazines dutifully pass the information along to the rest of the world about what it will soon be wearing.

One thing certain in the world of fashion is change. It's the nature of fashion to be always new. New fashions are the delight of the very rich who can afford to keep a constantly updated wardrobe. And new fashions are the lifeblood of the fashion industry itself.

Paris originals may not be within the reach of the average person, but shifting fashion trends affect us all. Is there anyone who hasn't stopped wearing this or that piece of clothing, not because it's gone out of style? Somewhere someone dictates that hemlines move up or down, or that lapels widen or narrow, and we rush to replace whole wardrobes that get old overnight.

Changing fashions affect more than just clothes, of course. We are consistently urged to look for new cars, furniture, appliances, and a host of sports and entertainment gadgetry. Keeping up with the latest fashions costs a lot of money, but failing to keep up has its costs, too – costs many people go into monetary debt to avoid.

Our culture's mania for constantly changing fashions is just one of its obsessions with outward appearance. In the same way, many people make snap judgments about the attractiveness, intelligence, and general worth of others on the basis of their possessions – how they dress, where they live, what kind of car they drive. None of these external things has anything to do with a person's real worth.

The system that lures people into debt by making them embarrassed to be out of style is not born of love. If we contribute to the evil of the system by making fun of someone who can't afford the latest fashions – or who simply chooses not to purchase them – then we display our own lack of love. The matter of fashion may seem like a small thing compared to the other great issues involved with love, but unless love takes on a practical meaning in the small issues of day-to-day life, it can't really have any meaning at all.

It's easy to blame the system for having created our problems, but the fact is that no system can survive without a lot of cooperation. The fashion industry survives because most of us really enjoy getting stylish new clothes. And while the big designers make a lot of us frustrated and poor from trying to keep up with their new lines of clothes, they also give us what we want.

Because most people know that they're judged by their appearance, they try to look as good as possible. This means different things to different people in different situations. Older men, for instance, may try to impress colleagues with expensive, well-tailored suits on the job – and on the weekends put on a jogging suit to look younger. Some women are interested in looking elegant, some in sporting a "natural" look, and others in adopting a more staid, businesslike appearance.

Younger people do more experimenting with the way they dress and look as they try to decide what's best for them, but because during this period of their life they are especially interested in physical beauty and sexuality, many of them choose clothes that will heighten their sex appeal.

Tight jeans and sweaters, short skirts, skimpy bathing suits – they're all designed to get attention, and they work. Some people have to fight a constant battle against sexual desires they know to be inappropriate, and their problems are only made worse by a multitude of temptations.

We could just write such people off as sick individuals. After all, we can't be expected to rearrange our lives for every nut that might be out there, can we? Well, we can't draw any hard and fast rules here, but if we want to live a life of genuine love, we'll have to take on some tough issues. We'll have to make some sacrifices of our own freedoms and preferences in order to accommodate the needs of some of the weaker individuals in the world around us.

Love means giving consideration to everything we do to see how it affects others whose lives we touch. It means putting the interest and needs of those others ahead of our own, even in all the little things in life, like the process of choosing the clothes we will wear.

A Game of Follow the Leader

Fashion exerts its power over more things in our lives than just clothes and other possessions. Fashion even shapes our behavior and attitudes to one degree or another. On a large scale, each culture develops deeply ingrained "fashions," or customs, on matters of faith, marriage, social interaction, and other aspects of life. Many oriental cultures, for example, venerate ancestors and show a great respect for their older people, while in the Western world youth is worshiped and the aged are often neglected. In many Eastern and Near Eastern cultures, marriage is not a matter of individual choice but of parental contracts, while in most Western cultures romantic love is considered to be the essential basis for getting married.

It wasn't so long ago that most girls worried a lot about others finding out if they lost their virginity before marriage, because that meant they'd have lost their reputation, too. It was the fashion for "decent" people to call girls like that *tramps*. These days, sex early in life is getting to be fashionable, and girls and boys both worry about the things people will say about them if it's discovered that they *haven't* lost their virginity.

There are lots of other fashionable attitudes we've developed, too, about smoking and drinking and driving and drugs. Every social grouping has its leaders and its followers, and the bottom line is that the leaders maintain the group's fashions by forcing the followers to go along.

Leaders actually have an easy time of it. There's a lot of social pressure backing them up. "Everybody else is doing it," they say; "what's the matter with you?" So a weaker girl might give in to the pressure to have sex because she thinks all of her friends have already done it, and she doesn't want to stand out as not being "with it," doesn't want to lose out on love. And a guy who might not otherwise push himself or his girlfriend into something he knows isn't right might be afraid that his friends will call him a "mamma's boy."

Leaders bring a lot of misery into the world by influencing so many followers to do things — often destructive things — that they wouldn't otherwise do. But leaders are like anybody else. They like other people to think they're tough, that they know exactly what they want and don't want, that they couldn't care less about the rest of the world. Of course they *do* care what the world thinks — that's why they work so hard to maintain their image, even to the point of lying about the things they've done (the stories you hear from them aren't all true by a long shot — they're just designed to get your respect). In this way, the leaders aren't much different from their followers: they're motivated by fears of what other people think of them, too.

Because leaders play such a big role in the lives of other people, they have to assume some responsibility for the situations they help to create. Most leaders refuse to accept responsibility for their actions, but the choice isn't really theirs. According to the Bible, the first murderer tried to get out from under his responsibility by asking, "Am I my brother's keeper?" The answer is "Yes, of course you are, whether you like it or not."

Leaders may think of their followers as weaklings — but at least that would give the followers an excuse: they're too weak to be responsible. But if leaders are as tough as they claim, they don't leave themselves any out. (This is not to say that followers are right when they try to get out of their responsibilities by claiming they're too weak. Nobody can talk himself out of responsibility for his own actions.)

To live is to be responsible — that's a plain fact. You can deny it or try to ignore it, but that doesn't change the truth of the matter. Love distinguishes itself by taking life seriously, by owning up to its own responsibilities to others. Living a life of genuine love is no easy task by any means. It takes a lot of strength and courage — to step outside of what fashion dictates to risk ridicule from the crowd for not going its way, to put somebody else's needs ahead of your own. Love is a lot tougher than all the tough-guy leader's grandstanding. But just imagine what the world could be like if it became the fashion to become genuinely loving toward one another.

Love and Sex

The Pleasure Principle

It used to be a taboo subject, something discussed only in whispers, but now everybody talks about it all the time. In fact, people might think you're a little strange if you don't discuss it openly and frequently. Discussion of every aspect of sex and sexuality has become such a national obsession that the suggestion is implicitly being made that life without regular sex is scarcely worth living.

There is no question that sex is important to people even without all the additional artificial hype it's been getting lately. The entertainment industry has always known it. Today's soft-pedaled smut on T.V. and hardcore porn in the theaters are both just slick refinements of the same sort of material people have always managed to produce in one form or another. And sex sells, of course. Advertisers know that nothing can beat it for making people more responsive to a product, whether it's an automobile or a box of laundry detergent.

The people who cash in on sex – advertisers, filmmakers, pornographers, and many others – meet with such predictable success for two reasons: first, most people have an instinctive interest in anything connected with sex to begin with; and second, a lot of people find their own sex lives unsatisfying and look to the fantasy world created by the sex merchants, with its beautiful men and women, for clues as to how things are supposed to be. But fantasy sex doesn't have any answers either, because it's lacking a key ingredient – genuine love.

Love and sex are closely related, even though a lot of people work hard to separate them. "Making love" has become a popular way of saying "having sex" – although in many situations where the phrase is used there isn't anything remotely like genuine love involved. What is usually present is that counterfeit kind of love we identified at the beginning of this book: self-love.

Sex is meant to be a loving union of two people, an expression of the love of each for the other. When you take love out of sex, you are left with two individuals seeking only to gratify themselves. The self-love of such people isolates them from one another and makes them cold and manipulative. This kind of loveless, recreational sex may yield the participants an occasional spasm of pleasure, but it also helps to plant the seeds of resentment, jealousy, alienation, and self-hatred.

Recreational sex concerns what we have rather than who we are. It puts the body at the center of the universe and suggests that physical pleasure is the highest good. Our society as a whole goes a long way in supporting this sort of philosophy. We glorify youth, we sell billions of dollars of cosmetics each year, we jump from one fashion fad to another, and we sell birth control drugs and devices in our supermarkets right along with breakfast cereals and soda pop.

Of course a life devoted solely to the pursuit of physical pleasure will become more and more meaningless as the remorseless years roll by. Cosmetics may hide our wrinkles, but they can't stop us from aging. A bikini may make men whistle for a few years, but there will come a day when it will only make them laugh. And the day will come, too, when birth control will no longer be necessary – nature will have put an end to fertility.

The advertisers would have us believe that youth is all there is to life, that we had better live it up while we can before we slip away into the world of laxatives and denture adhesives. They are in essence telling us that we are only worthwhile as pleasure machines. But they're wrong. There is another way.

If we choose the path of genuine love, it won't matter anymore if we aren't physically beautiful, because we will develop a beauty that won't fade with age or accident or any other circumstances.

The most beautiful in the world.

But what about her love for the world? Isn't she like a stone which, when it falls into the water, creates steadily bigger circles of doubt, hatred, jealousy, and inferiority feelings?

She is surrounded by her rivals, who are seldom noted for their whole-hearted agreement with the judges of the contest. In the next circle we find her relatives and friends. And in the outer peripheries, far from the glare of the spotlights, are the many, many girls who feel magically gripped to try their own luck, or who bitterly shut themselves off from the world because they do not have what it takes.

Maybe she doesn't have a perfect figure, and she hardly has time for make-up, and no man ever turns around to stare at her. But she does have perfect hands for helping people in trouble, perfect ears for listening to the difficulties of others, and perfect eyes for seeing where there is a need. The question is only which you wish to be: Miss World, or a Miss for the World.

The answer to that question will have a lot to do with what the world of tomorrow will ultimately look like.

Loneliness is a terrible thing. Solitary confinement is one of the worst punishments that can be imposed on a person. And most of us know from personal experience how unpleasant it is when friends or family give us the silent treatment because of something we've done. Nobody likes to be lonely.

Of course it's also true that not everybody who's alone is automatically lonely. We all like to have some time to ourselves every now and then. Some people even prefer to live their lives alone, and we should respect their choice. But the fact of the matter is that most of us feel a deep need for the sort of fulfillment that only another person can provide. We *need* love.

The search for somebody to love can get pretty complicated, though. Meeting others and getting to know them better is a difficult task for a lot of people – especially when it comes to dating. The dating game seems to have all sorts of unspoken rules that put pressure on people to act in artificial ways toward one another. Some people date for reasons that don't have anything to do with love: they just want to create an impression of popularity, to impress their friends, or to find some sexual release without any personal commitment.

People are attracted to one another by all sorts of things, but our first impressions are almost always shaped by the appearance of the other person. There's certainly nothing wrong with that – it's a part of human nature – but it can be destructive if it becomes an end in itself. If men and women never get beyond the point of viewing one another solely as objects that can be used to satisfy their needs – social, psychological, or physical – then they condemn themselves and their partners to empty, loveless relationships.

Sex can be a rich, fulfilling experience if it is the expression of the emotional wholeness two people feel together, of a commitment they have made to give themselves to one another in genuine love. But when sex is anything less than that, it can only serve to drive a wedge between people, locking them into the private world of their own pleasure. People who engage in sex just for the kick, who only seek the gratification of self-love, cheat themselves out of something much more valuable, and in effect wind up not loving themselves very well. Only love directed outward ever really benefits anyone.

Love and Marriage

The Promise of Love

A wedding picture: two people so much in love that they hardly think of anything but each other. Even so, their lives together have hardly begun, and their love has a lot of growing to do, too.

What will grow in their new life together – a little bit of heaven, or a living hell?

Most newlyweds believe in a heaven on earth, believe their love will be able to handle anything. They may be right. If their love is genuine – if they are more interested in their partner's happiness than in their own – they might well be able to face anything together. But if each is caught up in his or her own happiness – if their love is merely self-love – then their dreams of a domestic paradise will begin to fade almost immediately.

Almost everybody seems to think that the success of a marriage depends on how compatible the partners are – how many interests they have in common, how they get along with one another's friends, their sexual compatibility, and so on. But while it's true that a certain amount of compatibility is important for a relationship, it's also true that no two people are ever completely compatible. And in any case, even people who have a lot in common can still get on one another's nerves, even to the point where they hate each other.

Genuine love does more to make people compatible than any random matching of interests ever could, because genuine love means putting the other person's interests ahead of your own – loving him or her as you love yourself – and that means perfect compatibility.

Before your wedding day arrives, you owe it to yourself and the person you love to ask yourself seriously what it is you're looking for in marriage. Only if you're more concerned with your partner's happiness than with your own can you be assured of getting what you're after. And if you can make the decision to stick with your selfless love, you will have taken a big step toward making the world a better place.

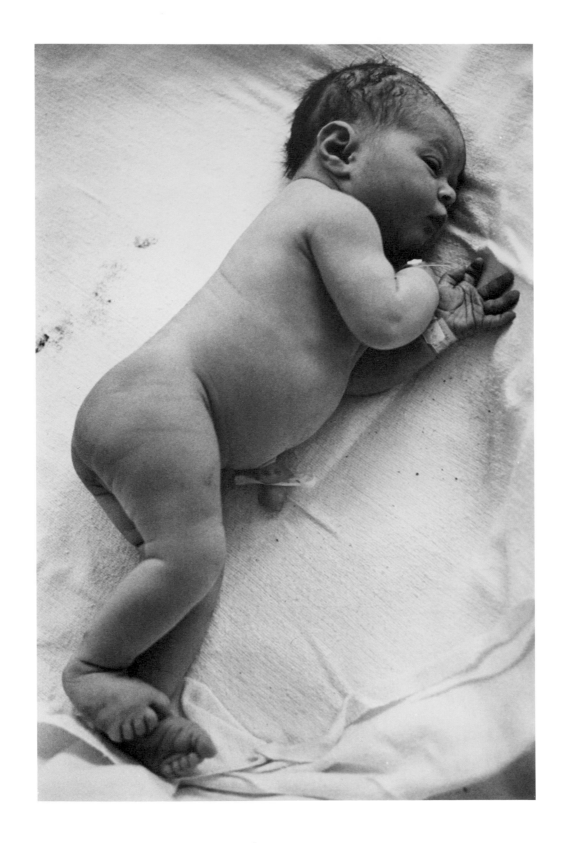

New Life for the Promise of Love

...Yet love still takes the risk of birth...

The Promise Broken...

For these people the dream turned ugly. They started out with hopes as high as anybody else's, but everything fell apart. They changed. Love faded. They drifted apart.

When she first met him, she thought he was such a nice, friendly guy. His friends still think so. But she's seen a different side of him. Under the pressure of bills and kids and the job, he turned mean. She tried to smooth things over. She tried to compensate for his frustrations by being extra nice. When he didn't appreciate her efforts, she started sticking up for her own rights. Sometimes she had to scream in order to be heard.

When he first met her, he knew she was something special. She was beautiful and warm and caring. She went out of her way to please him. But after they were married, she was always after him to spend his money on one thing or another, always coming to him with news that something was broken or worn out. *She* was getting worn out, too. The girls at the office were more considerate ... and younger.

Now they both consider divorce the best answer. Irreconcilable differences is what their lawyers will argue, but they're both convinced that they just had the rotten luck to get hitched to a loser. When a relationship goes sour, it's human nature to look everywhere but inside yourself for a place to pin the blame.

Love and marriage are big responsibilities. A couple may think that divorce will get them out from under those responsibilities, but they are ignoring the impact they've already made on the world with their actions. Their kids, if they have any, will have been robbed of one important chance to learn about the difference that genuine love can make in the lives of individuals and the world as a whole.

Here are two people who have lived one full life together. They, too, started out with nothing but love. The fact that they're still happy today is not the result of simple good luck.

They went through a lot of awful situations together – two World Wars, the Great Depression in the thirties, and a lot of personal trials, illnesses, and disappointments as well. It's easy to look at them now and chalk up their successful relationship to luck, but it isn't so. They spent their lives adjusting their own wants and needs to make themselves compatible to one another.

During the Great Depression, he lost his job, and his first concern was that he wouldn't be able to care for her properly anymore, wouldn't be able to give her the food and clothing and housing he wanted her to have. And she grieved for him, because she knew how much it hurt him to be forced into the helplessness of unemployment.

When war came and he had to fight, both worried again – she because of the danger he had to face, and he because she would have to face her own hardships all alone. And on, through sicknesses and pain, they stood by one another in genuine commiseration without complaint for personal inconvenience, and they grew old together.

They taught their children without ever having to say a word about what it means for two people to genuinely love one another. And by their example, they made it possible for their love to spread out into the world, because that's the way the world gets changed: not by clever politicians or peace rallies, but by individuals coming to see the truth about love, one by one.

Love and the Automobile

Because people are made the way they are, just about all of us spend our lives trying to satisfy two competing urges. Because we're all individuals – unique in all the world – we go to all sorts of lengths to set ourselves apart as one of a kind, to establish our own personal freedoms and independence. On the other hand, because we're social creatures as well, most of us feel a fairly strong urge to fit in with other people, usually people of our own age and interests. Both of these urges are perfectly natural – but, like most natural things, they can be ruined if we don't handle them properly.

We all know people who will do anything to get attention. Little kids will throw temper tantrums or hold their breath till they turn blue. Older kids will try to be the class clown, always cracking jokes or making fun of people. Some kids become bullies, pushing everybody around and generally making people feel rotten wherever they go. The adult world has its tantrum throwers and practical jokers and bullies, too, of course – and when adults engage in this sort of behavior, it's even easier to see how childish it really is.

But I think you'll admit that we all engage in little attention-getting activities every now and then, and it never really seems childish when *we* do it – at least not to us.

One of the greatest devices we've come up with for getting other people's attention is the Great American Freedom Machine – the car. Equipped with all sorts of lights, a horn, and a muffler (maybe a modified muffler?), this two thousand pounds of brightly painted steel, driven by a roaring power plant, can really make people sit up and take notice when it takes off in a cloud of burning rubber or comes barreling through a yellow light or squeals to a stop at an intersection.

People are transformed by the cars they drive. Some shy people become noisy and reckless when they get out on the road. Conservative people start taking all sorts of crazy risks. For teenagers with their first license in their pocket, the car becomes a great way to get out from under their parent's thumb.

Cars are so terrific because they can help people – especially young people – to fulfill both of the two basic urges we're talking about: they help to set us apart as individuals by giving us all sorts of freedom; and, as everybody who's been to high school knows, they also provide us with an important key to getting into society. But cars also make it awfully easy to go overboard in our attempts to be free and to be accepted.

Taking on Traffic

Maybe it's happened to you. You're driving along in heavy traffic and somebody who's obviously impatient gets behind you and starts tailgating, hanging right on your bumper and edging toward the center line, looking to pass. So you slow down a little – because nobody's going to pressure *you* into going any faster than you want to.

Or you're heading down a busy street and a car pulls out right in front of you and then just crawls along, backing up traffic behind you. You get so mad at the Sunday driver that you'd like to push him in a ditch.

Or you're out on the interstate and somebody passes you and pulls into the lane right in front of you, forcing you to slow down.

People can take on whole new personalities when they get behind the wheel of a car. Some people respond to the pressures and annoyances of traffic by laying on the horn, some by flooring the accelerator and taking chances. How many of us respond with love?

Maybe all this talk about cars and traffic seems to you as if it's drifted pretty far away from the topic of love. But the thing about love is that it is only really important in the specific situation of everyday life. We can theorize about love, refine our definitions, and argue about the fine points till doomsday, but unless we put love into practice in our lives, it will all be useless.

It's easy to see how mankind's refusal to learn the lessons of love brings about the tragedy of military conflicts. But we're far less inclined to pay attention to the fact that more people have died on America's highways than have died in all of her wars put together. We call them auto *accidents,* but is it really accidental when a tailgater plows into another car's rear end, or when somebody rolls his car when he's going twice the speed limit, or when a drunk crosses the center line and hits an oncoming car head-on?

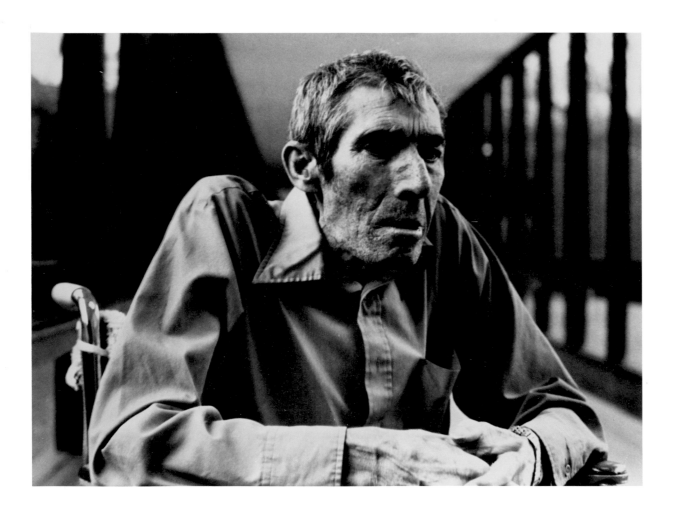

Life in the Slow Lane

The world moves at a faster pace now than it used to. The automobile is just one of the many things that have speeded up our lives. We're used to supersonic aircraft and fast-food restaurants and film that develops in sixty seconds. We're so used to all this speed and convenience, in fact, that we've begun to resent anything that slows us up. Old people don't move as fast as young ones do – and in a culture that already glorifies youth at the expense of older people, that's just one more strike against them.

What's your attitude toward older people? That they don't bother you as long as they don't get in your way? A lot of people seem to feel that way. If they had their way, all the old people of the world would be packed away into retirement homes where they wouldn't hold up tee-off times at the golf courses by hobbling around the links so slowly, or slow up the check-out line at the super-market while they fumble for change, or clog the highways with their crazy driving.

Even some people who really get down on bigotry and racism in the world still manage to get fed up with old people. Maybe it's because it's easy to talk about loving your fellow man regardless of race, creed, or color, but it's not so easy to demonstrate genuine compassion in the face of a frustrating situation.

It's an important lesson to learn, though. Someday, we all surely hope, we'll live to be what other people will consider old. We'll have to face some loss of our former strength and agility and general health. We'll have to live in a world made smaller by the loss of a regular income and by the death of our friends and family. We'll have to face a world that isn't very generous toward people our age, too, and we'll need love then more than ever.

Our lives are all of a piece. If we want to love others as we love ourselves, we must learn to love older people as well, whatever their annoying faults may be, for someday we, too, will be old.

Payer à son personne – it's a French proverb meaning "Give by giving yourself." If you want to show your love to older people, it's going to cost you more than just money. You're going to have to work to bridge the gap that our whole culture has helped to dig between the young and the old. You're going to have to give of yourself – but love never involves anything short of that.

Love and Sports

It's How You Play the Game

As a nation, we're crazy for sports. We can't get enough of them. Baseball, football, soccer, hockey, basketball, tennis, golf, track-and-field competition, even figure skating, yacht racing, and arm wrestling – if we're not out there participating, we pay to watch somebody else.

Sports has become a big-money, high-pressure business. The professionals and the owners both rake in millions of dollars yearly, but only a very few can make it to the top, and for most of them the job is so brutal and exacting that they can't hope to stay at the top for very long. In an environment where small failures can lead to enormous monetary losses and ruined careers, one of the first casualties of all the pressure is usually the principle of good sportsmanship.

Even with the current interest in physical fitness, not everybody is participating in sports, of course. Some simply aren't physically able to run or jump or toss a ball. But even if we aren't well-coordinated or strong enough to be good athletes, we all have the ability and the opportunity to be good sportsmen.

Good sportsmanship is a state of mind. It involves consideration for the other person – in essence, putting people ahead of points. It doesn't do you much good to win a game, after all, if you lose your self-respect doing it, and that can easily happen. Fierce competition makes many people forget about anything but winning. Whether it's World Series baseball or just a quiet game of checkers, too many of us adopt the attitude summed up by Vince Lombardi when he said that "Winning isn't everything – it's the only thing."

Bad sportsmanship, like any other kind of behavior, seldom remains confined to one area of our lives. If we learn to be bad sports on the playing field, we'll be just that much more prone to be bad sports any other place we have to deal with people. The constant urge to be number one is the same in principle whether it involves parents yelling at their kids to win at Little League baseball games, or families yelling at the breadwinners to get ahead in business. It's the same whether it involves the sometimes lethal and unnecessary roughing that some pro football players resort to, or the bloody fighting that street gangs get mixed up in. It's the same whether it involves a tennis pro who disputes every call against him and holds up the game with tantrums, or the international negotiating teams who get hopelessly hung up on silly points of protocol and never get down to the business of calling a halt to the killing.

There are also people who give up the fight to be number one in conventional ways because they feel the odds are stacked against them for one reason or another. Sometimes these people try to win in other ways. They're the ones who keep the radio blasting all the time in the middle of an otherwise quiet park or campground, driving the other visitors crazy. They're the ones who hang out on street corners to bug other people as they walk by. They're the ones who squeal their noisy cars through residential neighborhoods, scaring pedestrians and parents half out of their wits. They're the ones who become bullies in the hope that fear will get them the respect they couldn't win any other way.

Competition without good sportsmanship ends up being an every-man-for-himself kind of proposition. Translated into the world at large, it only serves to pull society apart: ideologies, nations, political parties, corporations, men, women, and children are all locked in a miserable war for supremacy. Less misery involves a greater challenge yet – the discipline of good sportsmanship, which has only one rule: love your neighbor as yourself.

Winners and Losers

During a period lasting several centuries, the elite of ancient Rome were entertained by the gladiators – professional combatants who fought to the death in public arenas. At the outset, this "sport" pitted criminals, slaves, and the hardened dregs of society against one another in bloody battle, but as the gladiatorial games became traditional, the jaded audiences demanded more variety. The unfortunates tossed into the ring included members of the aristocracy, exotic animals, dwarfs, and Christians. The Christians were the least entertaining of the victims, since most of them died without even attempting to injure their foes.

Today, most of us are repelled by the idea of organized murder serving as a public entertainment. And yet, our appetites are not really so far from those of the ancient Romans. We still enjoy seeing one football team maul another, still pay millions to see one prizefighter beat another senseless, still get a thrill out of watching a race car explode in some spectacular accident. Perhaps it's just that the Romans were a little more honest about acknowledging their bloodlust.

Our culture's overriding, single-minded interest in the winners of events also underscores our links with the Romans. It's easy to point to the gladiatorial games as being criminally cruel to the losers, but are we any less guilty when we casually murder the spirits of the people who lose – when spectators sneer at the losing team, when players gloat openly about the defeat of opponents, when parents put down their kids for not being winners?

In the world of sports there will always be more losers than winners. As long as we insist on cutthroat competition, on winning at all costs, we will only work toward making the majority of people miserable. If sports are going to be mentally as well as physically healthy, we must learn that the same rule applies in games as in the rest of life: love your neighbor as yourself.

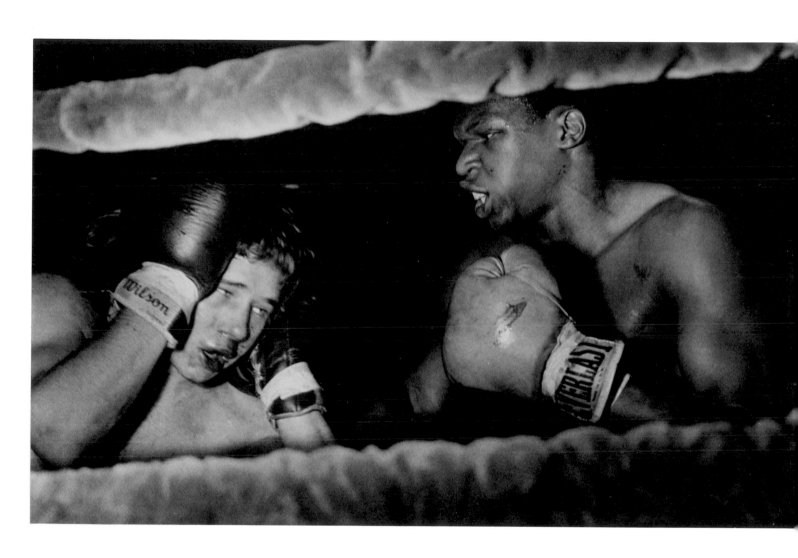

Love and Politics

The year was 1919, and the nation of India, then still in the grip of British rule, was in a state of turmoil. Revolutionary groups throughout the country were threatening to deprive England of one of her biggest colonies. In response, the British Parliament passed the Rowlatt Acts, legislation that gave the colonial government emergency powers to deal with revolutionary crimes and conspiracies. The response in India was outrage and agitation that quickly turned into violence and bloodshed. In the midst of the turmoil, a new leader stepped forward to urge a doctrine of nonviolent resistance. His name was Gandhi.

He was not unknown to his countrymen. He already had a reputation for his political activities in South Africa, where he lived from 1893 to 1914. The 150,000 Indians living in the country at that time were refused many of the rights enjoyed by more privileged citizens. Gandhi organized his countrymen into concerted resistance toward the oppressive government.

But Gandhi's methods of resistance were something new and startling. He convinced his followers to give up the standard tools of revolution completely. Without guns or knives – without even so much as a clenched fist – he and his people set out to face their oppressors.

Hundreds were arrested, including Gandhi himself. All went without a struggle. As time went on, it became apparent that if there was anything criminal about the struggle, the blame lay with the government. Facing scorn from the whole world, South Africa eventually backed down and conceded rights to the Indians.

Gandhi brought this same philosophy of nonviolent resistance to his native India in 1919. There, too, he was arrested along with his countrymen on more than one occasion. Through it all, he had the courage and the will to pursue his goal of independence, even though many of his followers gave up along the way, deciding to place their trust in more time-honored methods of violent revolution.

When India finally gained its independence from Britain in 1947, the country bore the marks of its long internal struggle: it was divided into two separate states, the one Hindu, and the other Mohammedan. On January 30, 1948, as he was ending the fifteenth fast that he had undertaken with the hope of easing the tension between these two states, Gandhi was gunned down by an assassin.

The world's best-known advocate of nonviolent resistance was senselessly murdered, but his message lives on. Martin Luther King, Jr., wrote the following words before he, too, met Gandhi's fate:

Gandhi was probably the first person in history to lift the love ethic of Jesus above mere interaction between individuals to a powerful and effective social force on a large scale ... It was in this Gandhian emphasis on love and nonviolence that I discovered the method for social reform that I had been seeking.

God is Truth

MKGandhi

Is there anybody who claims to love the people more than a politician?

Politicians never seem to tire of telling the world about themselves – about how they got into politics because they were tired of seeing the common man get pushed around, cheated, and deceived, especially when they have the solution to his problems. They want to assure you that with enough time – and enough money – they'll be able to usher in a new era of unprecedented prosperity, progress, and peace. Are you ready to believe that any political organization holds the key to utopia?

"If I have the gift of prophecy and can fathom all mysteries and all knowledge, and if I have a faith that can move mountains, but have not love," Paul tells us, "I am nothing." Before we put too much faith in the politician's ability to move mountains of social ills, we would do well to consider whether he is motivated by love.

Judging by election campaigns, it seems fair at least to conclude that politicians don't have much love for one another. It's a rare race for office that contains no mudslinging or dirty tricks. And apparently it's the next thing to political suicide to concede that your opponent has any good ideas at all. Every party organization seems just as sure that the opposition will bring disaster as they are that they themselves have all the answers. It makes you wonder how any politicians can claim to have the interests of *all* the people at heart when they've got such low opinions of their opponents and their supporters.

How often hasn't political concern for the masses come down to giving them what's good for them, whether they like it or not – for instance, when the British government assumed control over most of India in 1858, or when the United States government forced all of its citizens of Japanese descent into internment camps during World War II, or when Khrushchev sent Soviet tanks into Hungary in 1956 to quell an anti-Communist revolution among the people who, he explained, didn't have the vision to see what was in their own long-term best interests.

Politicians deal mostly in words – words that don't always have any connection to the real world of actions. To get votes, candidates will promise the moon, to the extent that people don't even expect them to keep their campaign promises anymore. It's all a game, and the players are practically interchangeable.

In recent years, Britain has had a conservative government, and it has been plagued by a weak economy and widespread unemployment. During the same period, France has had a liberal socialist government, and it, too, has been plagued by a weak economy and widespread unemployment. Regardless of the political philosophies they hold, nations all experience pretty much the same troubles because they are all populated by people who are pretty much alike.

To make the world a better place, we first have to make a change in the people who live there. Only if we learn to love each other as we love ourselves will things begin to get better. That doesn't mean we can't stand up for our own opinions and convictions; it means that we should want to be as concerned about the next person's right to hold *his* convictions as we are about our own.

Bread and Circuses

"Give them bread and circuses and they will let you do as you will."

That was the accepted political wisdom in ancient Rome as the Empire began its long decline, and it was sadly accurate: the masses were satisfied with little more than material goods and a quota of entertainment. The same thing is true of many societies today as well, although it is no longer fashionable to think of the citizenry as being *given* such things by a governing authority, benevolent or otherwise. Rather, we claim them as our *rights*.

Political theorists have haggled over the best way to ensure humanity its rights for as long as people have been joining to live in communities together. Today's global map is a patchwork quilt of nations each of which is convinced that it has found the best way for people to live together, but nowhere do you find a society in which everybody is satisfied with the way things are run.

All of the various political philosophies that have been tried – capitalism, communism, socialism, despotism, and others – wind up producing virtually the same sorts of inequities. No matter who cuts the pie, the pieces are never quite the same size – and even if they were, it wouldn't satisfy all the people. No political philosophy can stop people from wanting a bigger piece of the pie.

It's sad but true that you'd have to look long and hard to find anybody who was willing to give up enough of his own belongings that everybody would have the same amount. Most of us are always worried about getting the short end of the stick. We're all for social justice and against poverty and suffering, but most of us would just as soon have the solution start with someone else. Just imagine what it would be like if we all were really as concerned about the next guy's welfare as we are about our own.

We're fooling ourselves if we try to pin the blame for all of society's ills on a given political system or its leaders. The real fault lies with individuals whose self-interest is so strong that when it comes right down to it they don't really want fairness or equity for everybody if it's going to cost *them* anything.

Love is the only answer in politics as in everything else, and love always costs us something.

Love, Money and Power

"Money can't buy happiness" – it's an old saying, and most people would say they agreed with it if you asked them. But when it comes to everyday living, they're more likely to show a preference for another old saying: "Money isn't everything, but it's way ahead of whatever's in second place."

In our culture, we tend to use money as a measuring stick to gauge a person's success, intelligence, talent, and worth as a human being in general. Rich people automatically get more respect and better treatment from others just because they're rich. Their money also gives them access to better health care, legal services, and educational opportunities. All things considered, most people would rather be rich than be right.

In and of itself, money isn't really all that captivating. Relatively few people are content, like Dickens' Ebenezer Scrooge or his cartoon namesake Scrooge McDuck, with merely being able to fondle the coins and bills themselves. For most of us, the great allure of money lies in the things that can be done with it. Cynics believe that there isn't anything on God's green earth that can't be bought with money. Even if we aren't willing to go quite that far, we'll have to admit that a startling array of things can be bought with cash. The bottom line is that in this world, money means power.

Money provides a powerful means by which we can satisfy the two basic human urges we discussed earlier – the desire to be free and independent and the desire to be socially accepted. Both of these urges involve the desire for control over people and events in our lives. To that extent, they have a direct connection to man's original fall into sinfulness as it is recorded in the book of Genesis: man couldn't stand the fact that God was more knowledgeable and powerful than he was, so he ate the forbidden fruit in the belief that it would make him more like God.

People have been engaged in that same kind of attempted one-upmanship ever since – if not with God, then with one another – and the results have been consistently tragic. Everywhere we look we see exploitation and conquest, oppression and warfare, murder and theft, backbiting and put-downs. The history of mankind is written in blood.

But of course to condemn human history is to condemn ourselves. Our heritage as a race is our heritage as individuals as well: there is a destructive competitive spirit within all of us. When as children we struggled against the authority of our parents, and when as adults we have rebelled against the constraints of society, we have betrayed our own often petty desire to crawl to the top of the heap. The more we struggle against domination by the others, the more we surrender to the control of that competitive spirit.

It's easy to point an accusing finger at the superpowers with their arms race, and at the Middle Eastern and Central American countries with their endless bloodshed, and at the big corporations with their cutthroat business tactics, but unless we begin to acknowledge that all of these problems stem from a desire for power in the hearts of *individuals* – in ourselves as much as in anybody else – we cannot hope to point the way to a solution.

You hear about them every once in a while – the old derelict who lived like a bum even though he had a fortune hidden in his mattress, or the workaholic executive who deserts his family to spend more and more time at the office, or the tycoon who spends his life feverishly adding more millions to the millions he's already got. These people are never satisfied because they never get enough money to buy everything they want: they never get enough power over the things they have to face in life.

That much is true of all of us – our struggle for power is always a losing game, because there's always something out there that's stronger than we are. Even those people who deny the existence of God can't deny the existence of accidents, disease, or that final unconquerable foe, death. The simple fact of the matter is that no amount of struggle for money or power does much to reduce misery in the long run; as we have seen, greed and the desire for power over other people actually does just the opposite, creating untold misery and suffering throughout the world.

The only way we can start to reduce all the misery in our lives and the lives of those around us is to stop giving in to our consuming desire for power, to stop trying to get up in the world by stepping on those around us.

When the United Nations organization was formed in the wake of World War II, a lot of people hoped that it would finally bring an end to the insane destructiveness of war. It has proved to be so ineffective in reaching that goal that many now consider it to be little more than a bad joke. The problem is that all the member nations view the organization as just one more forum in which they can throw their weight around, one more platform from which to jockey for more power.

Power will not bring peace. Power will only bring the desire for more power. Christ told us how to achieve peace if we really want it: "Love your neighbor as yourself."

Love and the Difference
One Person Can Make

A Matter of Life and Death

Toward the end of the Second World War, a fighter plane was shot down over the jungles of Burma in southeast Asia. The two pilots managed to parachute from the aircraft before it crashed, but they had a rough landing. One of them broke both of his legs.

Despite the circumstances, the two men were happy just to be alive and together. But of course it wasn't long before they started thinking about how far it was to the nearest help and how dangerous the jungle that surrounded them was. It was inevitable that they started thinking that they might have been better off if they hadn't managed to bail out of their plane.

Nevertheless, they pulled themselves together, fashioned some makeshift splints for the injured pilot's legs, and set off for help. Five months later they staggered into an American war camp, the one lashed to the back of the other.

By all reasonable standards, neither one of them should have survived the 148 days in a hostile tropical jungle. Only the fact that they stuck together saved them — and this not just because they could take turns sleeping and keeping watch, but because each man's constant concern for the other kept him from collapsing under the strain of his anxiety for his own wellbeing. In a very real sense, the selfless love of each man helped to save both of their lives.

In the winter of 1854-55, the allied armies of England, France, Turkey, and Sardinia pitted themselves against the Russian army in one of history's most bungled and monumentally death-dealing conflicts. We know it today as the Crimean War.

Before the winter had even begun, the two armies had accumulated twenty thousand casualties, but as the cold began to come in earnest, the soldiers, ill-equipped and poorly fed on both sides, began to succumb to raging cholera as well as enemy attacks. More than half of the Allied armies fell victim to disease and the elements, and in one city alone the Russians lost more than 102,000 men. Men sent to such medical facilities as were available often found situations more horrible than what they had left.

Newspaper dispatches relayed detailed stories of the gruesome horrors of the war to the British public. One of those who was moved by them was Florence Nightingale, a daughter of the British aristocracy who had years before chosen to enter the field of nursing rather than lead the ordinary social life of a woman of her class.

She reached the Crimea in November 1854 with a staff of thirty-eight nurses just as a flood of hundreds of casualties began arriving at the hospital in Scutari. The awful condition of the soldiers – badly maimed in fighting and deathly ill with cholera – was matched by the awful conditions of the hospital, which was woefully unsanitary even by the standards of the time and place.

She set out immediately to fight not only the pain, disease, and filth, but also the military command, which hadn't invited her to come and resented her interference. Determined, she fought on, often working twenty-hour days. Eventually the effort paid off: in February 1855, the hospital's mortality rate was forty-two percent; within four months it had been cut to only two percent.

The effort cost Florence her own health – she was in bed with fever for twelve days herself, and felt its effects for the rest of her life – but she continued to serve in the Crimea until the last of the British left in July 1856.

She returned home to find that the press had made her a popular heroine. A huge sum of money had been collected for her throughout the nations, but she didn't use it to fund an early retirement. Instead, she used the money to build and staff a nursing school, in which she also taught, devoting all of her resources to the improvement of health-care services, especially in rural areas.

She died in London in 1910 at the age of ninety, but her life remains as an enduring example of the incredible things that can be accomplished by an individual motivated by love for her neighbors.

Many people know this man's name even if they don't recognize his face. He established a hospital in Labaréné, a small city in what was then French Equitorial Africa and is now the nation of Gabon not a very good way to become famous, but then that's not what he set out to do. He only wanted to help people develop what he called "reverence for life," but in doing so, he became one of the greatest pioneers in the area of foreign aid.

He was a brilliant scholar who gave up a very promising academic career to work among black Africans in an era when racist hatred of blacks by whites was stronger and much more open than it is today. His name was Albert Schweitzer.

Schweitzer built his hospital during the period between the two World Wars, and in the course of his life there he gained an intimate understanding of the people he served. The key to his success in crossing cultural boundaries was that he offered his help with no strings attached. He was not interested in payment of any kind – not wealth, or fame, or adoration, or power. His obligations all came from the love he felt for others, and he sought to fulfill them without political scheming or personal glory.

In the many years that have passed since his death in 1965, the almost legendary quality of Schweitzer's self-sacrifice has grown – but there have also been those who have attacked his record. They point out that his famed hospital was little more than a hut. Chickens scratched in its dirt floors. Relatives and families of the patients came in to cook and care for the patients. Compared to even the most modest hospitals in the "civilized" world, Schweitzer's facility was dirty, unhygienic, and sloppily run.

Schweitzer was, of course, aware of the contrast between his hospital and those he had left behind in Europe. He believed, though, that he could not really serve the people of another culture effectively until he understood where they were coming from, what they were really like, and if he set up a hospital that was a replica of the ones he was used to, it would only have insulated him against getting to know his new patients. Who among them could have come to trust a strange white doctor with unheard-of procedures in an environment that was itself totally alien?

Schweitzer may have sacrificed some small amount of medical efficiency by choosing the relatively primitive facilities he did, but in doing so he took a major step forward toward providing genuine help to people who might well have rejected help offered in any less loving manner. He was careful to attend to the dignity as well as the health of his patients.

PART III
WHERE
DOES GOD
FIT IN?

The Search for Love that Lasts Forever

God Is Love

The Christian church is made up of all the people throughout history who have come to believe in the things that Jesus said about himself and the world. A big part of Jesus' message was devoted to the importance of selfless love, as we have seen, and yet it's pretty clear that the church has fallen awfully short of living up to that standard. Throughout the ages, people have criticized the church – quite rightly so – for failing to actually live by the beliefs it professes. Others, however, have gone one step further and rejected the idea of faith in Jesus on the basis of what some of his followers have done. This sort of criticism is unfair.

Jesus knew that the total commitment to love he asked of his followers is no simple undertaking, even if its rewards are great. Again and again, he warned people that living a life of genuine love involves an enormous amount of self-sacrifice and suffering, because the world is always ready to take advantage of the person who offers love freely. He also predicted that many people would be attracted by the prospect of a life lived in selfless love and then would fall away from it as soon as it started costing them something.

The Christian church is made up of all sorts of different people, all at different stages in their commitment to Jesus' teachings. None of them has reached the sort of perfect commitment that Jesus himself had, although they all profess a desire to reach it. More and more, conditions in the world are providing an acid test for each Christian's commitment. Sadly, some don't pass the test at all, and none of them does all the time.

The current state of world affairs threatens to undermine everyone's beliefs. Humanists – people who believe in the ability of humanity to overcome all of its problems on its own – are surely shaken by mankind's resolute insistence on creeping ever closer to the brink of nuclear annihilation. People who trust in God and try to follow his commands are greatly tempted to turn their backs, too, on the many who seem to be bent on destroying them. They are hesitant to reach out in love to a world that only wants to snap their arms off. But people who pull back from a total commitment to love show that they have not understood Jesus' teachings.

Jesus came to introduce a special kind of love – a love that would extend to everyone, even his worst enemies. "Love your enemies," he said, "do good to those who hate you, bless those who curse you, pray for those who mistreat you…If you love those who love you, what credit is that to you? Even 'sinners' love those who love them." If we choose, as most people do, to love some people, hate some people, and ignore the rest, we will only help to perpetuate the misery in this hate-filled world. Only a complete and genuine love for all of our neighbors can overcome the endless barriers we all build between ourselves and others.

Members in most churches contribute a whole lot of money every year to what they call *evangelism* or *missions,* so that the "Good News" of Christianity can be brought to unbelievers around the world. This makes sense, because these believers all claim that their faith is very precious to them, and they want very much to show their love for others by passing the precious gift along to them. But in many cases, their concern seems to end when they plunk their money into the collection basket.

It's the case in many churches that members are far more willing to pay money for missionaries to go out and preach than they are to say anything themselves. Many are more interested in foreign missions than in local ministries, too. And if by chance an unbeliever or stranger should happen to stumble into one of their worship services, it's far too often the case that that person would be treated like someone with the plague rather than be welcomed with open arms. Maybe the visitor wouldn't be tossed out on his ear, but more than likely he'd get the message that he wasn't welcome.

How is it that church members can be so cool and standoffish? It's just that they haven't fully learned the lessons they claim to have learned from Jesus. Jesus saw the same problems in the religious people of his own day – like the man who gave him dinner and then was disgusted by the prostitute who poured perfume on his feet. He was sad to have to say it, but Jesus simply couldn't condone such behavior, and he told these religious bigots that they were farther away from God than the thieves and whores they looked down on were.

The love that Jesus brought into the world is difficult to practice in our own lives. It goes against human nature. Even people who sincerely want to love others as Jesus taught have problems and often fail. But just because his followers are imperfect is no reason to reject either Jesus or his teachings. Some people use the church's failures as an excuse to avoid the burden of love themselves – but in doing so they only compound the failure by robbing the world of the love they could contribute. However much we may want to deny it, we all have a responsibility to love our neighbors as ourselves.

Christians are people like anybody else, afraid of the big responsibilities of love, afraid to stick out their necks to help strangers. As they mature in their faith, they gradually grow into a fuller commitment to love. That may explain some of the lovelessness in churches today – it's just that they're made up of immature Christians – but, of course, it's no excuse. As Jesus pointed out on several occasions, people who claim to be his followers have a special responsibility to love others, and they will be judged more harshly for their failures.

Some people have said that it seems like there are as many different denominations as there are Christians in the world. It's certainly true that the Christian church is broken up into a lot of different pieces. How can this be, if all of them claim that they're just trying to follow Jesus?

Part of the problem, once more, lies with the fact that the church is made up of ordinary people, and even the best-motivated, most sincere people in the world will disagree about the best way to get something done. The many different branches of Christianity were each born out of groups or individuals who thought they saw a better way to follow Jesus and then felt committed to put that better way into action.

You can look at the Christian church in either of two ways: as a splintered chaos of bickering factions, or as a diverse family of people all of whom are trying to serve God as best they can. You can make a good case for either point of view.

The Christian church has experienced divisions from the very beginning of its existence. Jesus' follower Paul addressed such a problem when he wrote a letter to a church that had formed in the city of Corinth not many years after Jesus' death. Believers there were arguing about who was most important, whose life was most like what Jesus wanted. Paul used a metaphor to point up their error: *The body is a unit, though it is made up of many parts…If the foot should say, "Because I am not a hand, I do not belong to the body," it would not for that reason cease to be a part of the body. And if the ear should say, "Because I am not an eye, I do not belong to the body," it would not for that reason cease to be a part of the body. If the whole body were an eye, where would the sense of smell be? …As it is, there are many parts, but one body.*

Paul was not specifically addressing the problems of the modern church, with its many denominations, in this letter, but even so, the principles he outlined can be applied to the situation. He is just saying that even in the church there is room for a *diversity* of expressions of faith so long as there is at the bottom a *unity* of faith in Jesus' teachings.

Paul's analysis makes sense. We rejoice in the diversity of nature, in the beauty of a multitude of different plants and animals, in an unending variety of different sights and smells and tastes and experiences. Too much uniformity can be deadening. And so, too, within the Christian church there is a rich variety of emphases and traditions. Some Christians express their reverence for God in quiet ceremonies and awesome cathedrals, others in loud, joyful ceremonies and simple clapboard buildings. Some stress emotion, some philosophy, some social action, but all genuine Christians are motivated by their love for Jesus and his teachings, and that is the source of the beauty in all of their diversity.

To the extent that the different branches of the Christian church argue amongst themselves, they have lost sight of Jesus' teachings. But we should never let the mistakes of the few serve as an excuse to exempt ourselves from living a life of love. If you believe in God, your place is in a church where you can feel at home.

Don't blame it on the Jews, Lord
Jesus; they didn't do you in.
They aren't the ones who bribed the
judge.
And the spit on your face did not
come from them.
They did not hit you till you burned
with boils.

Don't blame it on the soldiers either;
they had nothing to do with the
sticks and hammers that rapped
you down.
The cursed logs of Golgotha were
none of their doing,
And they were not the ones who
threw dice for your robe.

It was me, Lord, it was me – I am
the one who did this to you.
I am the tree that knuckled you
under.
I'm the real reason you are tied up.
I am the nail and the crack of the
whip,
The bloodthirsty crown that
surrounds your head.
For all this has happened, alas!
because I, I have let you down.

— based on a poem by
Jacobus Revius
(1586-1658)

Throughout this book we have tried to search out the ways of love. The more we look, the less love there seems to be. The world as a whole seems to be smothering in self-interest and open hostility, with the occasional act of genuine love appearing like a brief flash of light in a long, dark night.

It's time to ask ourselves again whether it's really true that God is love, and what that could mean for a love-starved world.

Our world is all of a piece. It's intricately constructed in a beautiful web of being that ties all living things together in interdependence. Human beings are spectacularly adapted to life on this planet, to its air and water, climates and food supplies. We are one link in a great chain, one part of a great mosaic that includes the oceans and mountains and plants and animals and each other.

Alone in all creation, mankind has also been given the gift of moral choice. People can search out what is good and bad, and to an incredible degree we can impose our will upon the planet to make it whatever kind of place we want.

The most significant choice that mankind has made is the choice to sink into all of the sins connected with self-love. The Bible tells us that the rest of the world was so carefully attuned to the needs and desires of man that in some awful way all of it was turned on its ear by man's resolute selfishness. When man turned from love to savagery, nature became savage as well. Because man got greedy and began competing to get a bigger share of the pie, all of nature became competitive, too. The result is that people have to fight nature to get what they want – and nature fights back.

All in all, there's a sort of grim justice to the human condition: whatever we toss at the world comes back to us again. We pump hate, greed, and carelessness into the world, and it throws injustice, poverty, and calamity back in our faces. We reap what we sow.

This is not to say, however, that as individuals we suffer in direct proportion to our evil. That sort of belief is put forth by some people, but it clearly isn't so. Some suffering may be a direct result of our actions – as when we get lung cancer from smoking too much, or sustain injuries from an accident caused by reckless driving – but there are also nonsmokers who get lung cancer, and accident victims who have been hit by reckless drivers even though they themselves weren't doing anything wrong. In fact, the Bible goes so far as to tell the story of one very good man – his name was Job – who suffered great losses and pains. His friends tried to convince him that he must have done something pretty awful to have been punished so badly, but he knew that he wasn't any worse than the rest of them, and he told them so.

Suffering doesn't come from some sort of angry God tossing down thunderbolts from heaven to punish sinners below. Suffering is the result of the choice made by the whole family of man to live a life of selfishness and evil rather than of love – it's the price we all have to pay for putting our own interests ahead of anyone else's.

It's no secret that the world is in a mess because of all the things mankind has done to it. We've turned the rivers and oceans into open sewers, we've sickened or killed off countless animals with pesticides and industrial wastes, and we've manufactured devices that can literally extinguish every last bit of life on the planet. Our history is full of senseless wars, our cities are full of brutal crime, and our brains are full of all manner of unspeakable sickness. A lot of good and beauty still surround us, but we seem bent on twisting all good things into worthless trash. Where does all this evil come from?

People have been pondering the causes of evil for as long as they've walked the earth, and they've come up with a lot of candidates over the years: government, parents, technology, fate, capitalism, communism, education, hormones, evil spirits, UFOs, fluoridated water – you name it. All of these suspected causes have one thing in common: they are all forced on us from the outside. But Jesus taught that it doesn't do any good to try to pin the blame for evil on some scapegoat out there somewhere. The real problem, he said, lies *within* us.

Jesus tried to get across to his followers that the cause of evil is something at the very heart of human nature: mankind's deep-seated, unshakable, perpetual, overwhelming self-love – what the Bible calls *sin*. Sin is the result of mankind's decision that it prefers self-love to any other kind of love. People gave up their close relationship with God and tried to go it alone fueled only by self-interest, and that decision helped to cut each individual off from the neighbor as well as from God. Locked into lovelessness by their own selfish choice, people have wandered through the world in misery ever since, never satisfied, never fulfilled, never whole.

Jesus came into the world to restore mankind's lost contact with God. He gave the simple formula for wholeness: turn away from sinful self-love and instead love God and your neighbor as yourself. It's a simple formula, but old habits are tough to break. Selfish people would rather do almost anything than give over their tiny worm-eaten lives to genuine love.

Generally speaking, the people who claim to follow Jesus are just as self-serving as anyone else. They're still full of their old human nature. Many will accept what the Bible has to say about sin, but then try to apply it to everybody but themselves. They use Jesus' teachings like a pair of glasses to inspect everyone else's sin, while the truth of the matter is that the Bible is meant to be used as a mirror in which each of us can get a better look at our own sins.

Unbelievers are just as self-serving as believers, but on the whole they're less hypocritical about it. They say to themselves, "If God exists, then either he or I must be good-for-nothing, and since I don't want to believe that about myself, God must be the guilty one. But any God who's good-for-nothing is worse than ridiculous, so even if he does exist, he's not for me." It's the oldest dodge in the world: somewhere, someone else is to blame, but not me. Don't try to pin the blame on me!

Because all of us are so crazy to avoid the blame for evil, we go to all sorts of trouble to make cases against the scapegoats we choose, and we usually back up our charges of guilt with a good dose of hate – racial hatred, anti-government sentiments, rebellion against parents. The cries of blame echo through all the gunfire and explosions, all the declarations of war and vows of revenge, all the threats and cutting remarks of history.

But the granddaddy of all scapegoats is still God. After all the nations have blamed one another, after all the citizens have blamed their governments, after each child has blamed his parents, and those parents have blamed their parents, and so on and so on, all the way back, the ultimate culprit is God: "If God really exists and he made this world, he should have done a better job of it," come the cries through the ages.

That's the reason so many people believe that it's such a bad joke to say that God is love: it robs them of the perfect scapegoat for their incredible burden of guilt.

If you become a parent, you and your spouse will have to make some basic decisions about how you want to raise your child. If you want to protect the child from the ravages of an evil world, you could decide to shelter it completely by locking it away and keeping it from reading or seeing or hearing anything about the outside world. Every once in a while you'll read in the newspaper about some parents who actually try something like that. Most people would agree that, far from being protected from evil, such children are actually exposed to an especially hideous kind of evil by their misguided parents.

The other option open to you as a parent would be to teach your children about the difference between good and evil and then do everything in your power to try to influence them to make good choices about the way they'll live their lives. Such a plan of action is, of course, risky. You can't make your kids' decisions for them, and you won't even be able to convince them what's best for them much of the time. You can only give them the best opportunities you know of to learn what's right, and then trust them to make the right decisions on their own.

God was faced with a similar set of options when he created mankind. The only way he could have made sure that people would live in harmony and peace would have been to create robots who had no choice in the matter. Instead, he made people free to choose which way they wanted to live. He tried to convince them that selfless love was the key to happiness and that selfishness would turn their lives into a living hell, and then he stood by them in love, hoping they'd choose to preserve the love they shared.

The fact that people chose – and still choose – the path of selfishness is not God's fault. He has tried again and again to convince us to turn our backs on evil and take up lives of love. Because he knows how beautiful things could be, the prospect of a world full of evil sickens him more than it does us. But he continues to love us enough to grant us our freedom to choose how we will live our lives, no matter how much we abuse that freedom, and in doing so he provides a continuing example of genuine love.

Maybe at this point you're saying, "Look, I'll agree God's not to blame for all the mistakes I've made. I'm willing to accept responsibility for my own action. I'm even willing to go along with the proposition that mankind is responsible for a lot of its own misery. I mean, after all, we did build concentration camps and drop the atom bomb on civilian populations. We're even responsible for most of our traffic fatalities. But what about natural catastrophes – the storms and floods and plagues? You're not going to tell me that I'm responsible for *them*. Nobody causes them, and nobody can stop them. If God is sending them as punishment for sin, then he's not only being cruel but arbitrary – I mean, how does he decide who deserves to be singled out? We've all got to die, but why do some people have to suffer so much first?"

Once again, the answer lies in the fact that God loves us enough to grant us the personal freedom of choice that we crave. We can only exercise our freedom in a world that provides us with real options to choose from. If the world were constructed so that we never faced any sort of risk, then we'd never be able to accomplish anything either, because there's almost nothing in our environment that can't be used to harm us in some way. Or God could have put each of us alone on empty worlds, in which case we might be safe from the hatred of others, but we'd also be cut off from any other sort of relationship. In order to have a potential for love, hope, glory, and all good things, we must also be open to the possibility of evil.

The willingness to accept responsibility is a measure of maturity, and it is a sign that we are maturing as members of the human family when we own up to the fact that our own selfishness is in part responsible for the sad shape the world is in. And if we are willing to shoulder our part of the blame for the world's suffering, we'll also be that much closer to alleviating its problems, because we'll be that much closer to learning how to love.

If you accept your responsibility, you won't have to waste your energy looking for scapegoats or shaking your fist at God. If you feel a personal pang every time you see someone else hurting, you won't need anyone to prod you into helping those who need help. If you can see that suffering is a burden shared by the whole family of man together, it will be that much easier to love your neighbor as yourself.

Love involves sacrifice, but it's more than worth it. If you've ever been loved, you don't need anyone to tell you that. As the whole world staggers under the agonies of hatred and indifference, as each individual walks his own lonely path through illnesses and pains, rejection and misunderstanding, on the way to the inevitable grave that is the great leveler of all men, it is the acts of love that stand out in the bleak landscape as the only really valuable experiences in life.

Love is the most precious thing we can have, and unlike anything else, the more of it we give away to others, the more of it we have ourselves. But as precious as it is, the love we experience is only a pale shadow of the genuine article that Paul described so beautifully:

Love is patient,
love is kind.

It does not envy,
it does not boast,
it is not proud.

It is not rude,
it is not self-seeking,
it is not easily angered,
it keeps no record of wrongs.

Love does not delight in evil but
    rejoices with the truth.

It always protects,
always trusts,
always hopes,
always perseveres.

Love never fails.

Consider Paul's description of love in the light of your own life, and you'll see that the things we've talked about in these pages hardly scratch the surface of what genuine love is all about. But you'll also see how powerful genuine love must really be if it can mean so much to us even in its watered-down human version.

There's no denying that it will cost you dearly to stick your neck out for love, but the dividends are invaluable – joy, contentment, wholeness – and the costs of living a life without love are immeasurably higher.

Without love, life is hardly worth living at all.

Having said that much, we could bring this book to an end, but to do so would be to leave a very untidy end indeed, because if that's the whole story, then it's better left untold. What good does it do, after all, to say that love is the only hope for the world if love remains beyond our reach? On a global scale, our best efforts seem to come to nothing – or worse than nothing. Nobody wants war, but to prevent it we build more deadly bombs and edge closer to war every day. In the middle East and Central America, people who hate war and oppression are taking up guns and killing each other in an insane self-defeating attempt to keep the peace. Even those opposed to violence cannot shake its grip. As Bertolt Brecht wrote,

Even the hatred of squalor
Makes the brow grow stern.
Even anger against injustice
Makes the voice grow harsh.
Alas, we
Who wished to lay the foundations
    of kindness
Could not ourselves be kind.

So the time has come to ask whether love is in the end just a pipe dream, and whether God's love, even if it is real, has anything to do with this world.

God's love first touched the world when he created it. He made a home of boundless beauty for his favorite of creatures, mankind. When people took over the household and began running it into ruin, when they told God that they neither needed nor wanted him around anymore, he could in good conscience have turned his back on them and left them to make their own way. But his compassion for his creatures was greater than a simple sense of justice, and he decided to go out of his way to show man the road that led back into paradise.

And that brings us, of course, to Christmas, the day on which we celebrate – amid all the rubble of evergreens and tinsel and wadded wrapping paper and eggnog and mistletoe and Santa Claus and T.V. specials and endless parties – the fact that God sent his son to earth to point the way for us.

Our culture does what it can to bury the incredible glory of that act of love. We blind ourselves with flashing lights, and deafen ourselves with tinny department store music, and dull our senses with Christmas cheer. We even send in substitutes for Jesus – flying reindeer, talking snowmen, ghosts, and street-corner Santas.

But the real Jesus came to turn the world on its ear. He brought a revolutionary new way of life. He came in love to change history, and he stands in a completely different category than any other reformer or revolutionary who ever entered the world: he was – and is – the son of God, as much God as the Father who sent him. He came with the power of God to change people's lives in ways that are beyond anyone else.

Jesus came to a world of people that didn't know anything about his radically different kind of love, to a world of people so lost in their own selfishness that they wouldn't have been able to live lives of genuine love even if they wanted to. If Jesus had been an ordinary man with that kind of message, he would have been able to interest a few people with it, but he would not have been able to give them the strength to change their lives. As the son of God, however, Jesus did have the power to change lives, and he still exercises that power today.

As the Bible tells us, during Jesus' years on earth he displayed his power and his love by healing people's diseases, both physical and spiritual, even raising people from the dead. The winds and waves obeyed him. Even the rulers of the time recognized his power in a dim sort of way – they considered it a threat. They saw that it could change forever the way of life they were used to, and being practical men of the world, born and raised in the worst traditions of human selfishness and evil, they took God's gift of love and nailed it to a cross and hung it up to die.

They only did what the world still does to love – they tried to stamp it out quickly, before it had a chance to spread. It didn't work any better then than it does today. Jesus didn't resist them in their attempt. He made the ultimate sacrifice, going so far as to accept the burden of their guilt, leaving them completely free to choose his love or not, just as they pleased. His love was so perfect that it survived the grave and has continued through the centuries to offer hope and the power for change to the unhappy people of a love-starved world. The love of God is stronger than death even yet for all who will accept it.

The great price has been paid to secure for *you* the freedom to choose how you will live, too. The choices are clear: the hell of lovelessness or the heaven of God's love. If you choose the latter, remember what is being asked of you as well as what is promised: "Follow me and love your neighbor as yourself."

Acknowledgments

Translator: Nick Overduin
Editor: T.A. Straayer
Associate editor: Carol Holquist
Graphic design: Dawson+Company
   Design/Communications, Inc.
Production: Wobbema Press, Inc.
Project manager: Rinck Heule

PHOTO CREDITS

Craig VanderLende:
   Cover, 3, 7, 10, 18, 29, 37, 44, 50, 59, 76, 80, 91
Neal Hayden: 4, 13, 23, 27, 46, 54, 79, 85, 89, 92
Union for Distribution of the Holy Scriptures:
   9, 32, 49, 64, 73, 74, 82
Multi-Media: 43, 53, 56, 66, 69
United Press International: 17, 20, 38, 63, 71, 86
The Image Bank: 14, 35, 76
Historical Picture Service: 61
ibid, inc.: 24 (top)
Dirk Bakker: 24 (bottom)
Marian Heule: 41
Steve Warner: 31

May the Lord Jesus bless all that is done to His glory.